HAL•LEONARD

GUITAR PLAY•ALONG®

DAVID LEE ROTH

CONTENTS

Cover photo by Neil Zlozower

Tracking, mixing, and mastering by Jake Johnson
All guitars by Doug Boduch
Bass by Tom McGirr
Keyboards by Warren Wiegratz
Drums by Scott Schroedl

ISBN 0-634-07925-5

Visit Hal Leonard Online at www.halleonard.com

T0058831

HAL•LEONARD®
CORPORATION
7777 W. BLUEMOUND RD. P.O. BOX 13819
MILWAUKEE, WISCONSIN 53213

Ain't Talkin' 'Bout Love

Words and Music by David Lee Roth, Edward Van Halen, Alex Van Halen and Michael Anthony

Am G5

1.

Ain't talk - in' 'bout love.

Just like I told you be - fore,

P.M. P.M. - - -| P.M. P.M.

Am G5

— yeah, be - fore._____ 2. You know you're sem - i good -

P.M. - - - - -| P.M. P.M.

2.

Am G5

Just like I told you be - fore _____ be - fore,_ uh, be - fore,_ uh, be - fore,_ be - fore.

w/ bar - - - - - - - - - -|

P.M. - - -| P.M.

*Hold bend while sliding.

Guitar Solo

Am G5 Am G5

w/ bar - - - - -|

let ring - -

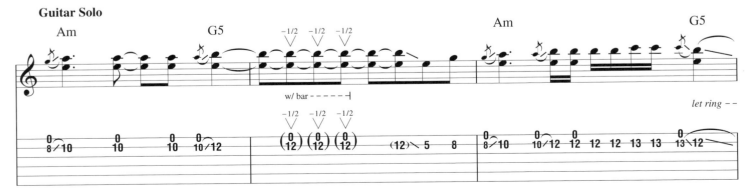

4

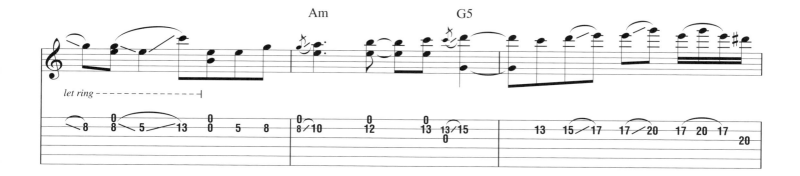

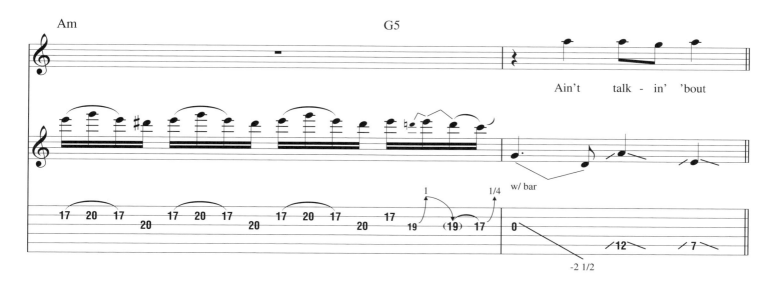

Chorus

*Lower vol. knob about halfway to produce a slightly distorted tone.

Interlude

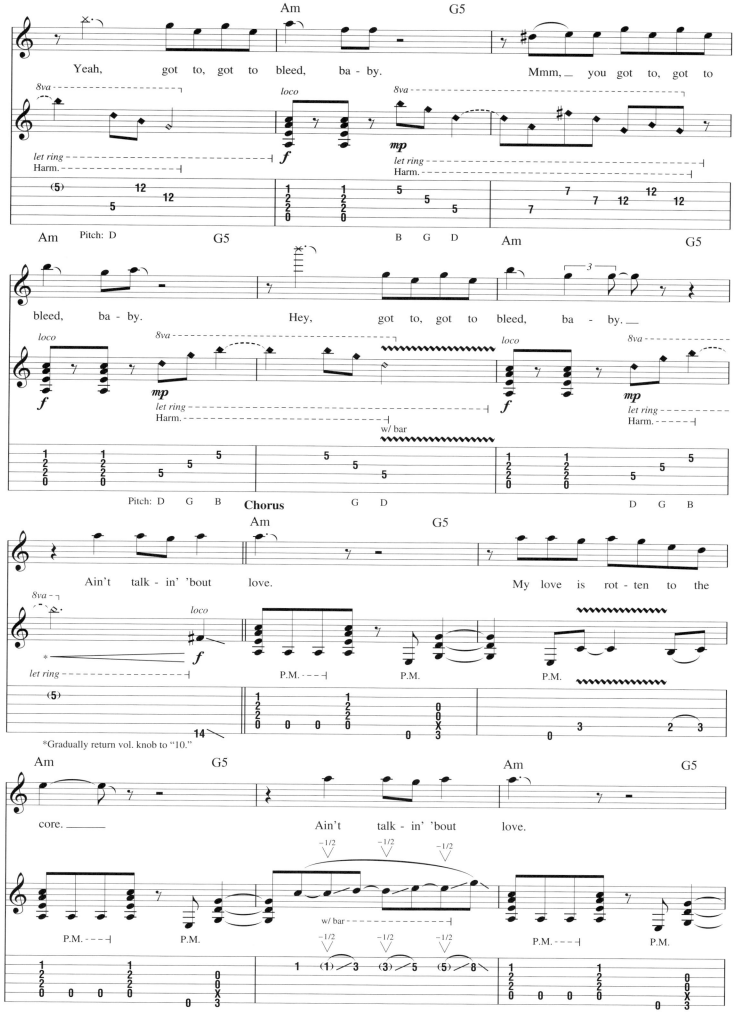

Guitar Solo

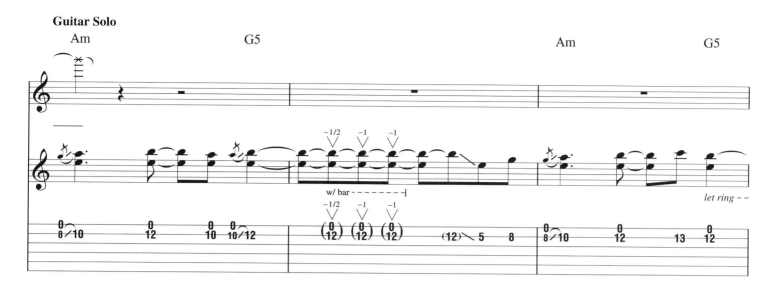

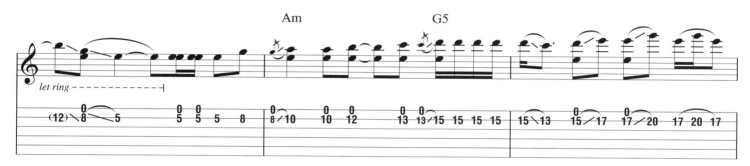

Outro

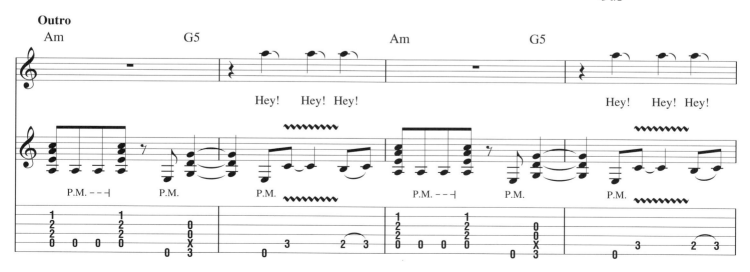

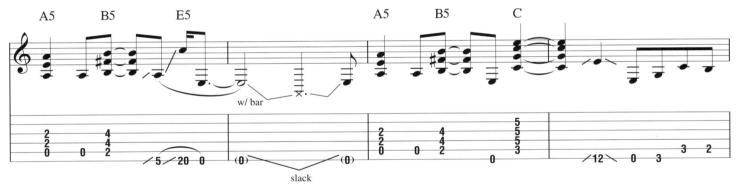

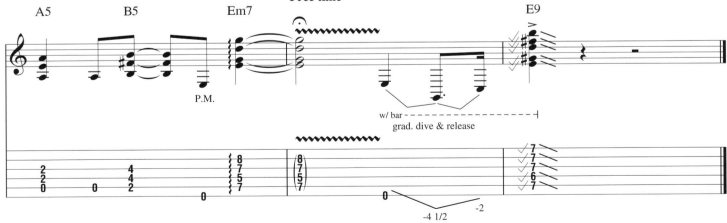

Additional Lyrics

2. You know you're semi good lookin',
And on the streets again.
Oh, yeah, you think you're really cookin', baby.
You better find yourself a friend, my friend.

Dance the Night Away

Words and Music by David Lee Roth, Edward Van Halen, Alex Van Halen and Michael Anthony

Tune down 1/2 step:
(low to high) E♭-A♭-D♭-G♭-B♭-E♭

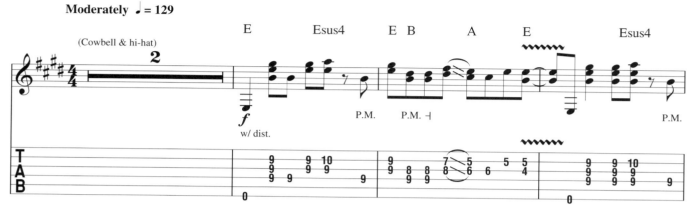

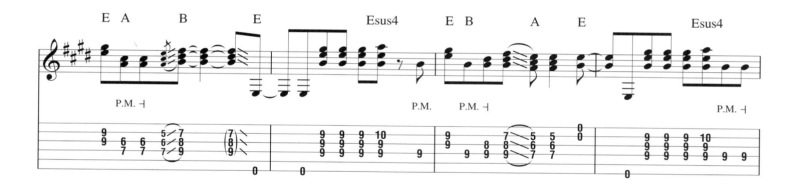

Verse

1. Have you seen ___ her? ___ So ___ fine and pret-ty. Fooled ___

Copyright © 1979 Diamond Dave Music, WB Music Corp. and Van Halen Music
All Rights for Diamond Dave Music Administered by Chrysalis Music
All Rights for Van Halen Music Administered by WB Music Corp.
All Rights Reserved   Used by Permission

11

me with her style and ease. ___ And I feel ___ her ___ from a-

cross the room. Yes, it's love in the third de-gree. ___

Pre-Chorus

Oo, _____
(Oo, ba - by, ba - by.

won't ya ___ turn your head my ___ way?

*Artificial harmonics produced by tapping strings 12 frets above fretted notes.

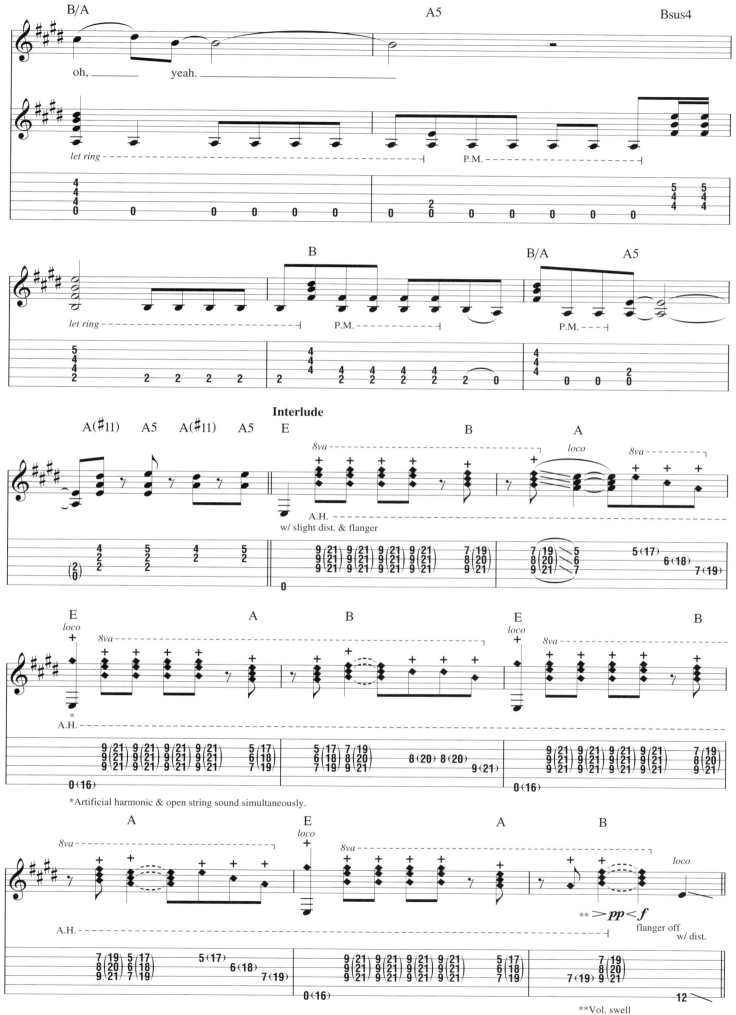

*Artificial harmonic & open string sound simultaneously.

**Vol. swell

Just Like Paradise

Words by David Lee Roth
Music by Brett Tuggle

Intro
Moderately fast ♩ = 136

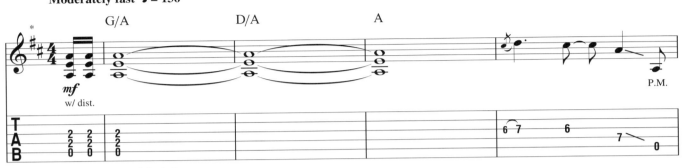

*Key signature denotes A Mixolydian.

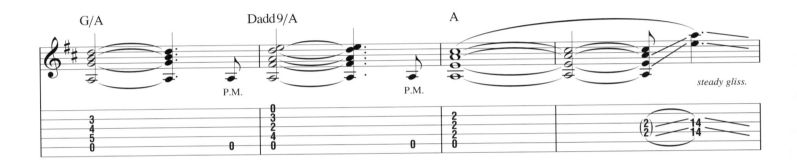

Half-time feel

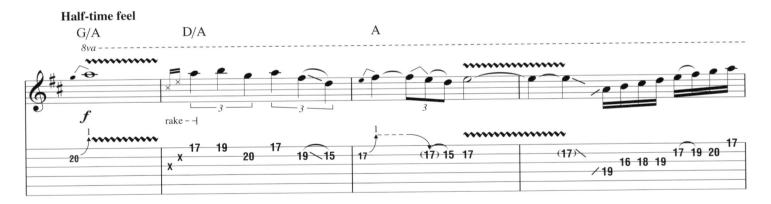

End half-time feel

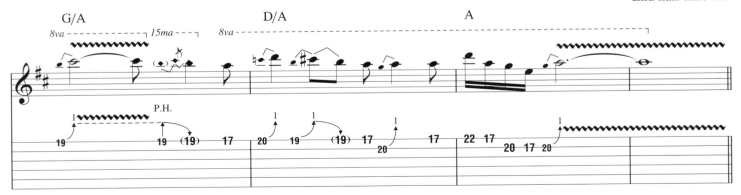

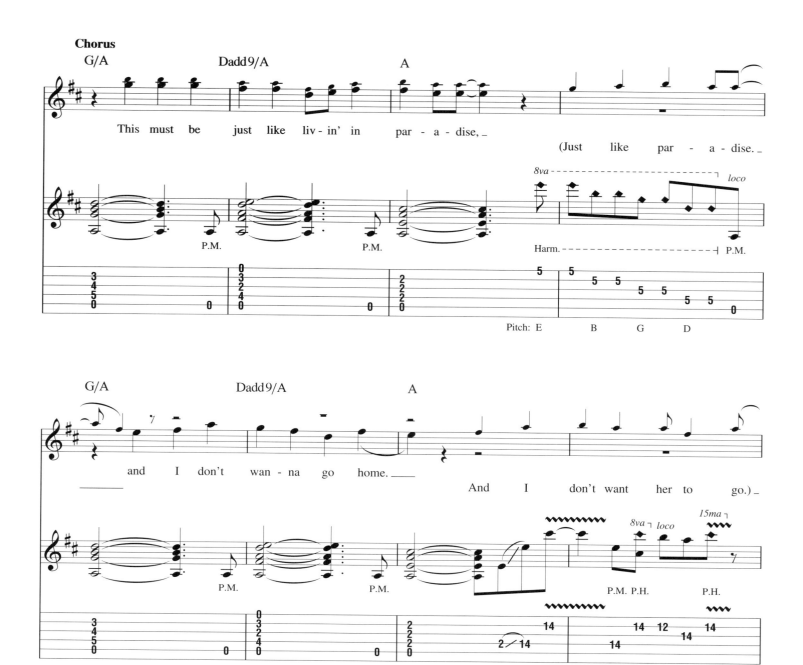

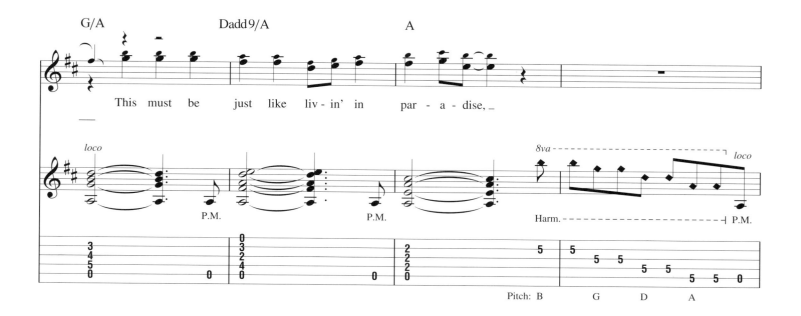

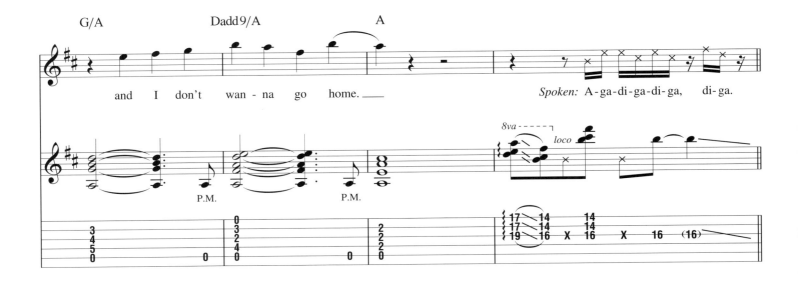

and I don't wan - na go home. ___

Spoken: A - ga - di - ga - di - ga, di - ga.

Verse

2. Suz - y, Suz - y, girl, for cry - in' out loud. ___ You got all ___ the right moves, ___ you make ___

___ me eat my heart ___ out ___ night - ly. ___ Oh. ___

(That's all ___

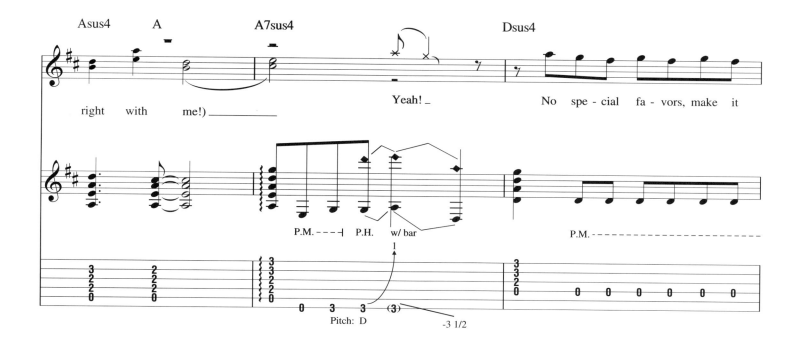

Pre-Chorus

Spoken: That's it, that's it.   Some folks say,   "Eas - y come __ is

mp
w/ clean tone & chorus
let ring -

eas - y   go." __   ..."But   one night ain't __ e - nough __
(And some folks say...) _

let ring - - - - - - - - - - - - - - - - - -

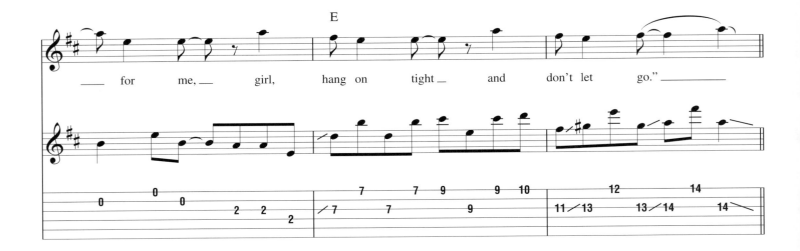

__ for   me, __   girl,   hang on   tight __   and   don't let   go." ___

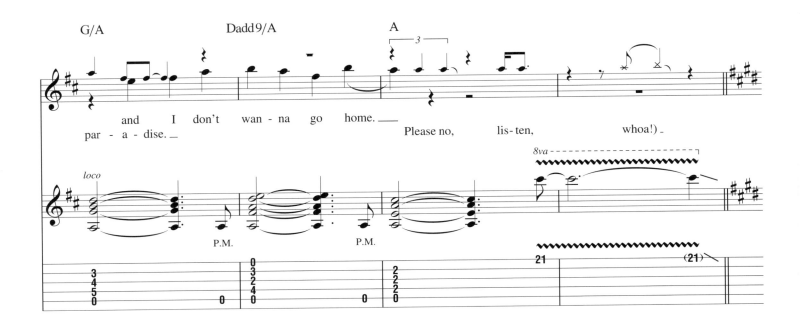

and I don't wan-na go home. ____
par - a - dise. ____

Please no, lis- ten,   whoa!) ___

Guitar Solo

(Huh,   huh,   oh yeah.

Ah, ____

Pitch: A#   B#   A#   B#   A#

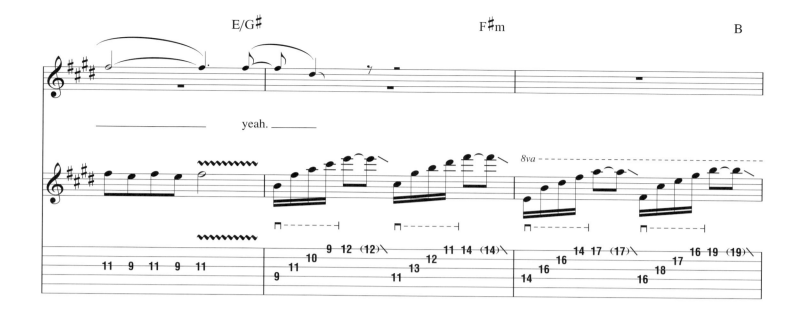

yeah.

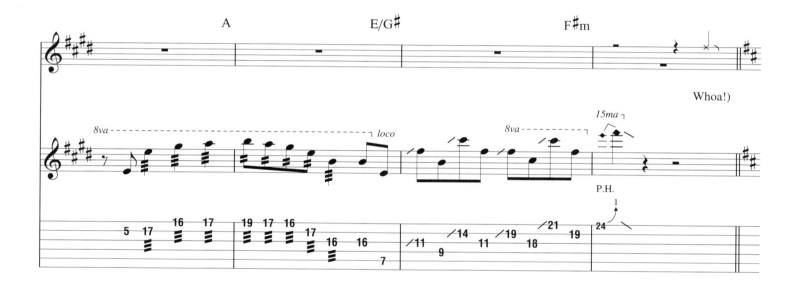

Whoa!)

Chorus

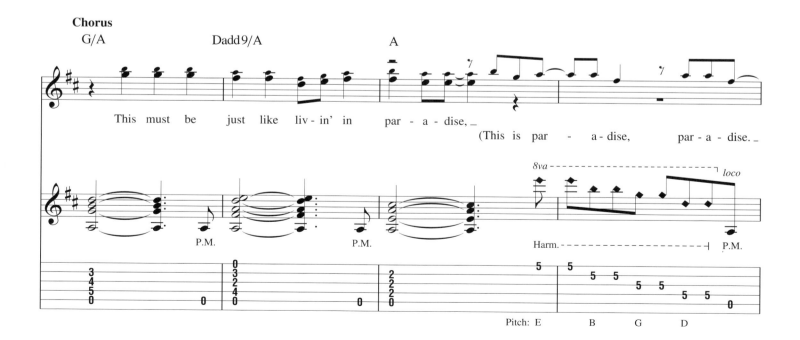

This must be just like liv-in' in par-a-dise,_

(This is par-a-dise, par-a-dise._

Pitch: E   B   G   D

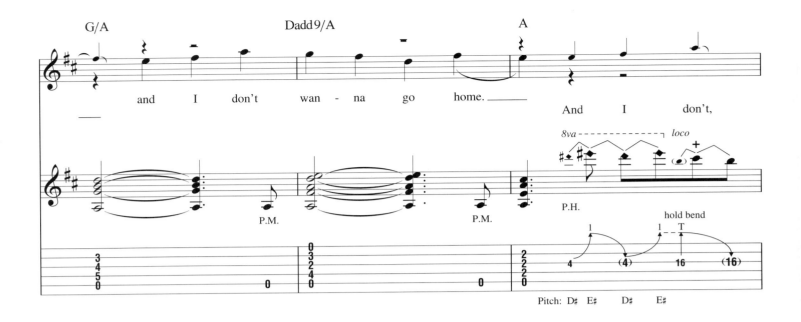

A Lil' Ain't Enough

Words by David Lee Roth
Music by Robert Neville

Intro
Moderate Rock ♩ = 126

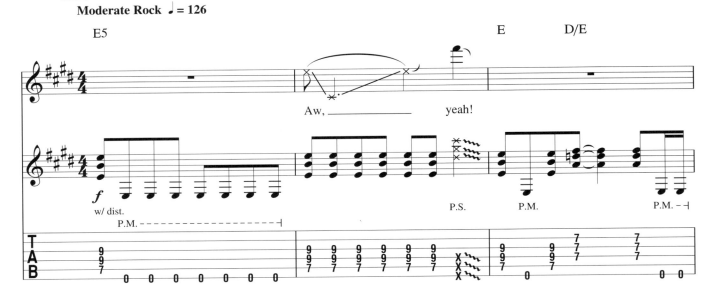

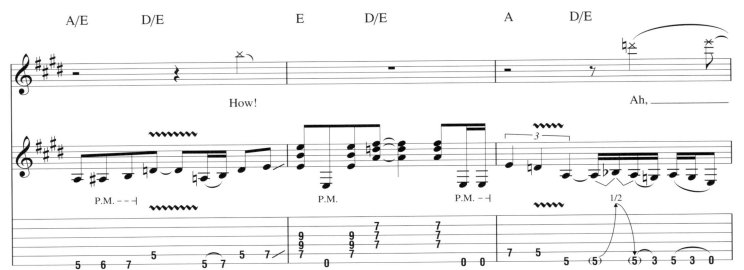

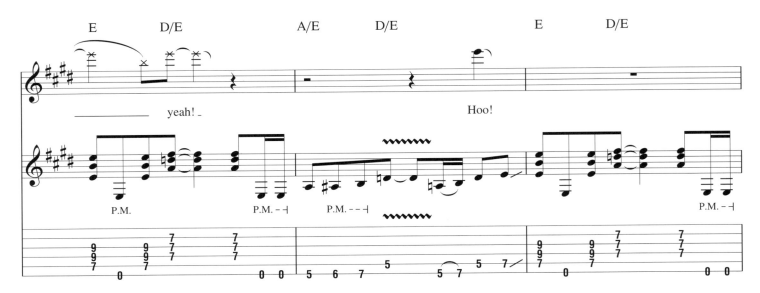

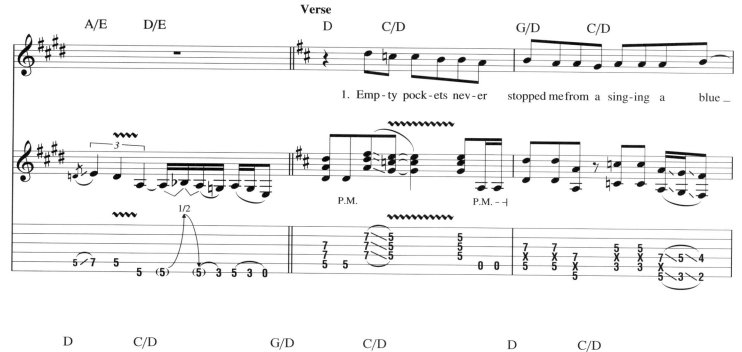

stay-in' 'round here takes pa - tience, it's like a full - time oc-cu-pa-

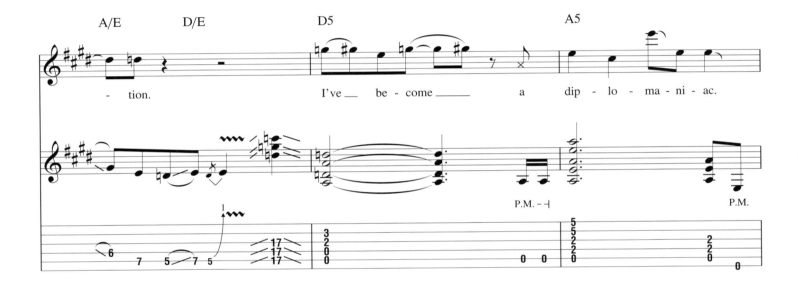

-tion. I've _ be - come _ a dip - lo - ma - ni - ac.

Yes, I did, _ ba - by. _ Hey,

Pre-Chorus

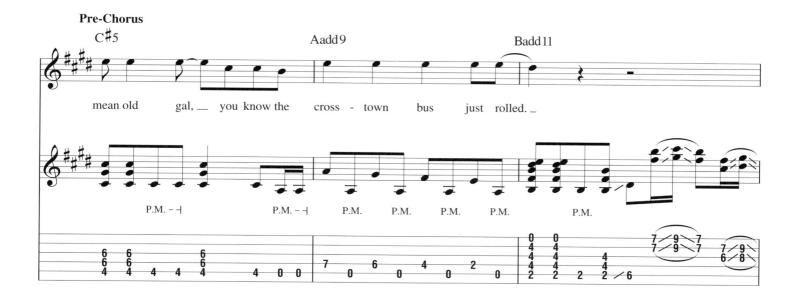

mean old gal, __ you know the cross-town bus just rolled. __

Yeah, I'm the same old num - ber, but we still got time to go, __

oh. _____ *Spoken:* Sing it, babe. __

Chorus

Whoa, I __ say ma - ma, liv - ing ain't a lux - u - ry, __ no. __

Oh. __ Whoa, I __ say ma - ma, and a lit - tle ain't e-

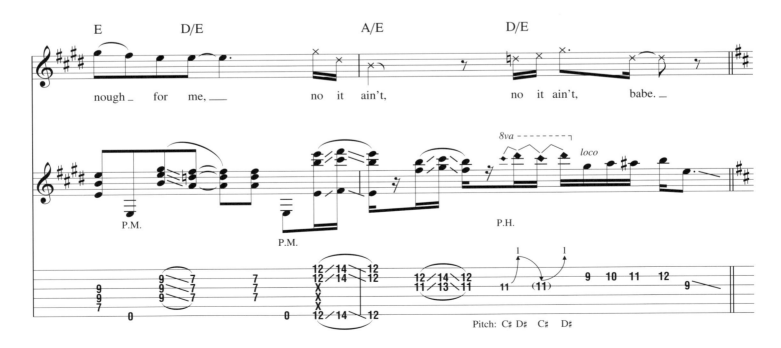

nough _ for me, __ no it ain't, no it ain't, babe. __

Pitch: C♯ D♯ C♯ D♯

2. Yeah, I'm be-liev-ing that you're need-in' your __ re-lax - a - tion, whoa. __

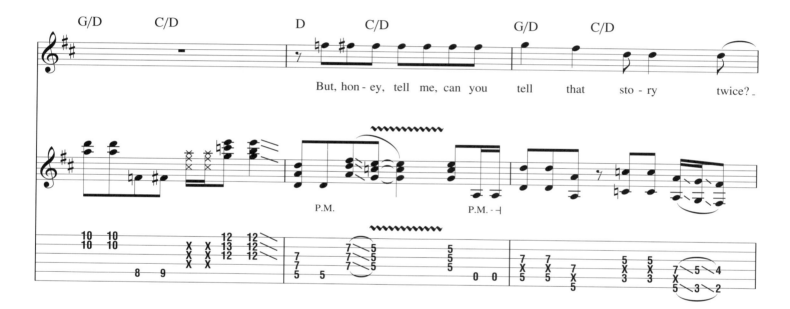

But, hon- ey, tell me, can you tell that sto - ry twice? __

I don't think __ so, ma - ma. 'Cause there's a func - tion at the junc-

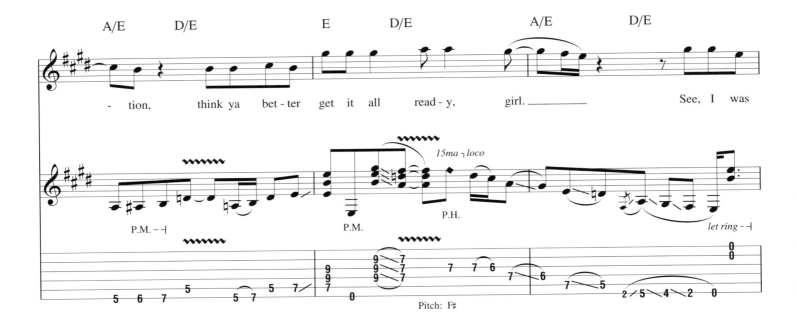

-tion, think ya bet-ter get it all read-y, girl. _____ See, I was

Pitch: F#

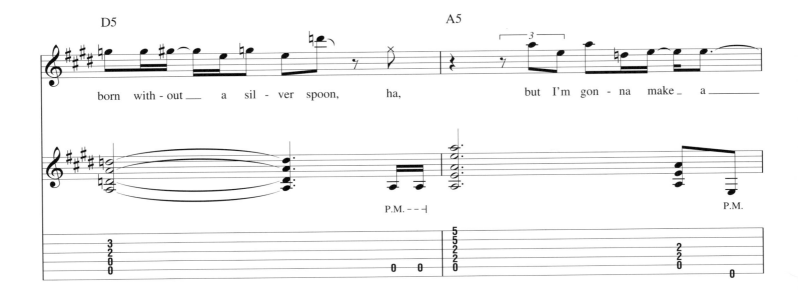

born with-out ___ a sil-ver spoon, ha, but I'm gon-na make _ a _____

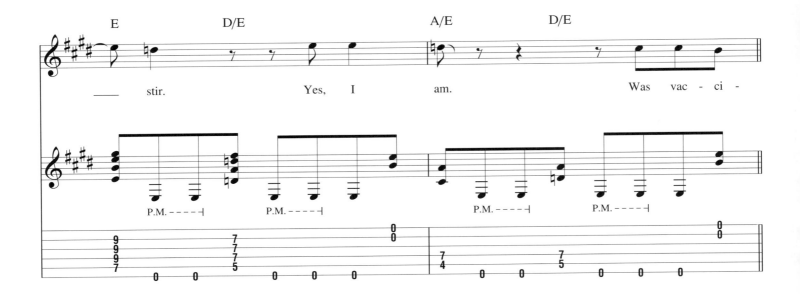

___ stir. Yes, I am. Was vac-ci-

Pre-Chorus

nat-ed with a pho-no-graph   nee-dle one   sum-mer break. _____   Oh! _____

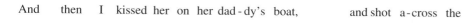

And   then   I   kissed her on her dad-dy's boat,   and shot a-cross the

lake, _____   and   I   was   sing-in' it! ____

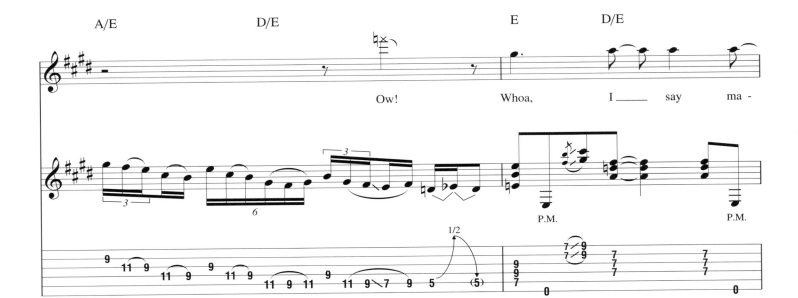

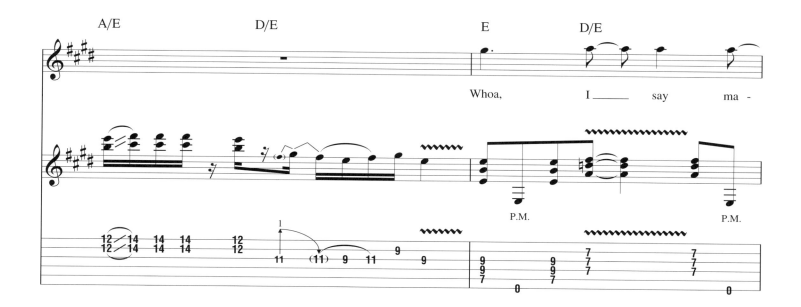

Whoa, I ____ say ma-

-ma, liv-ing ain't a lux-u-ry, ____ no. ____

— Ah, ____ no. Whoa, I ____ say ma-

Pitch: A

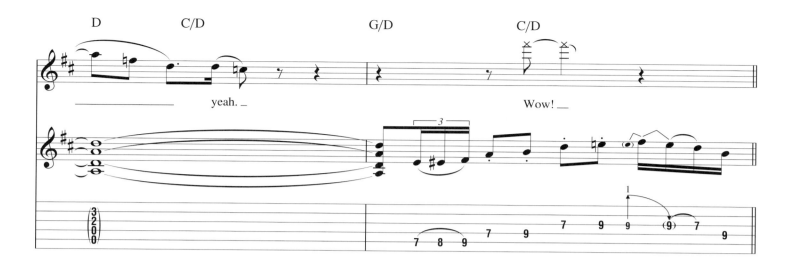

yeah. ___ Wow! ___

Guitar Solo

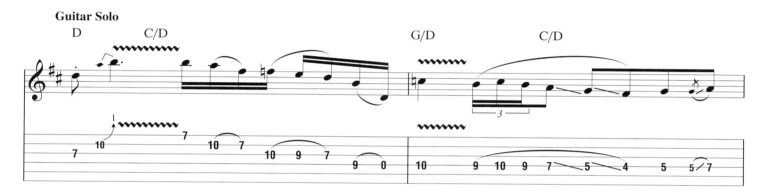

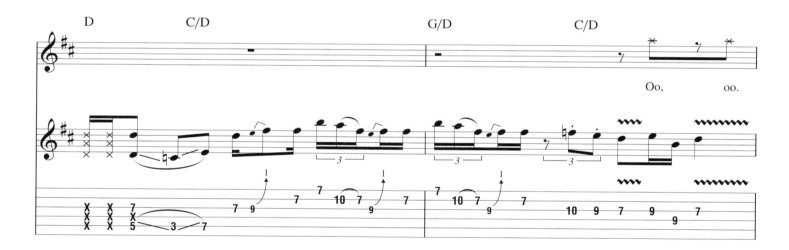

Oo, oo.

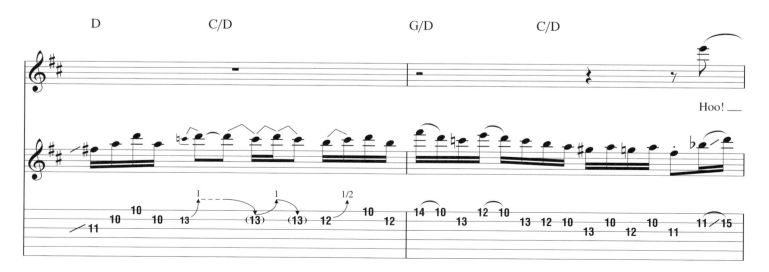

Hoo! ___

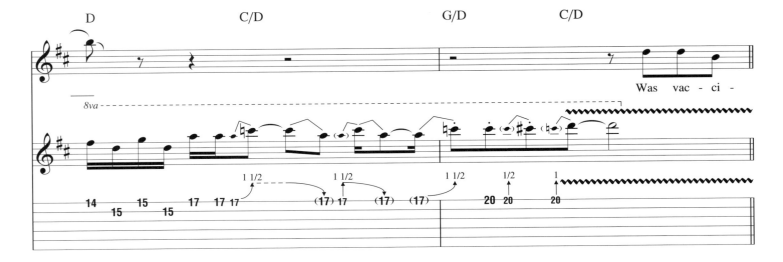

Was vac - ci -

Pre-Chorus

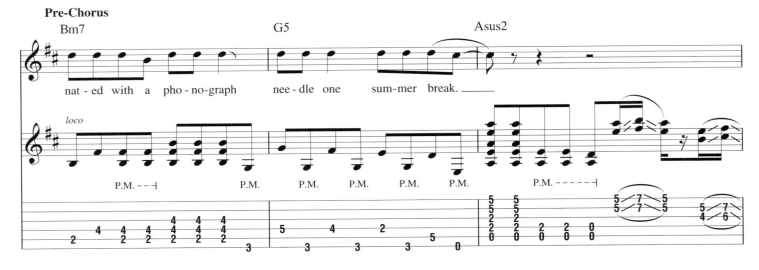

nat - ed with a pho - no - graph nee - dle one sum - mer break.

Same sum - mer that I kissed her on her dad - dy's boat,

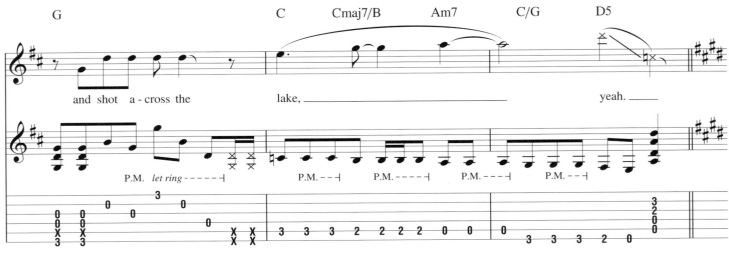

and shot a - cross the lake, yeah.

Chorus

Whoa, I ___ say ma - ma, said a liv-ing ain't a lux - u - ry. ___

Oh! ___ Whoa, I ___ say ma - ma, I say lit - tle ain't e -

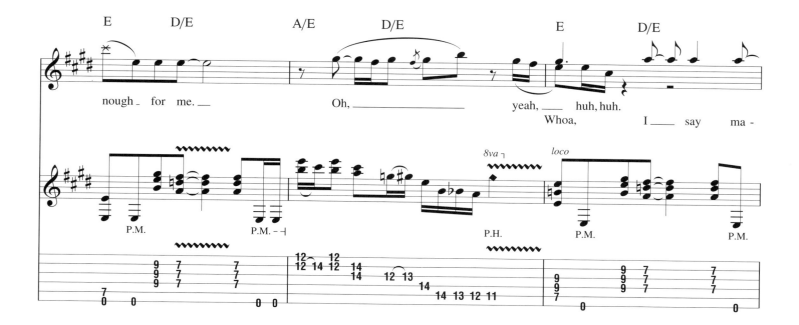

nough _ for me. ___ Oh, _____ yeah, ___ huh, huh.
Whoa, I ___ say ma -

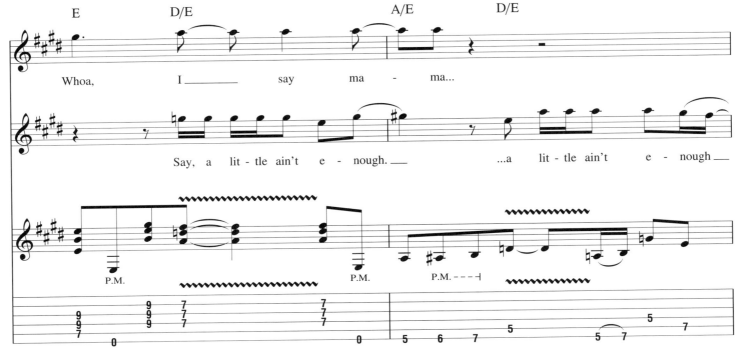

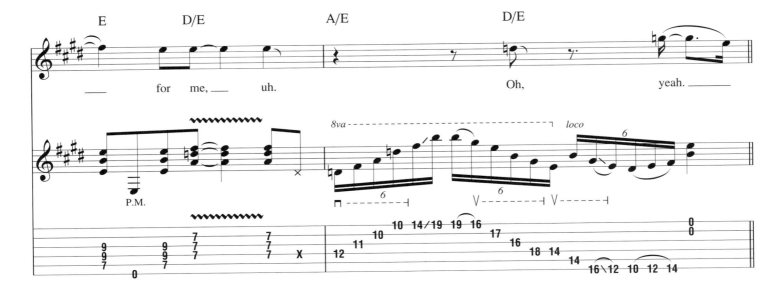

46

Outro

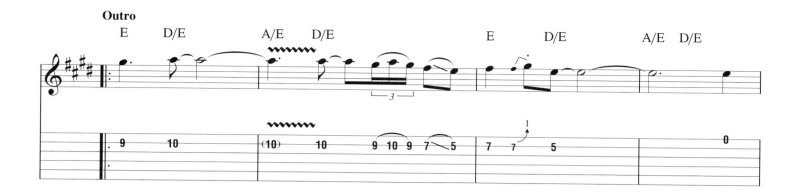

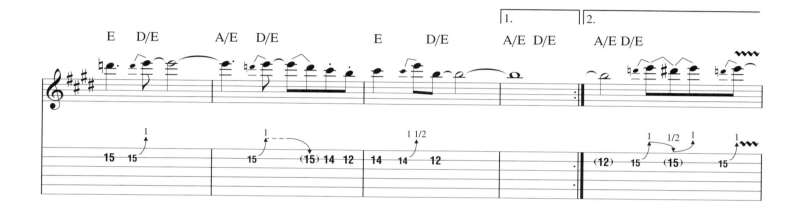

Free time

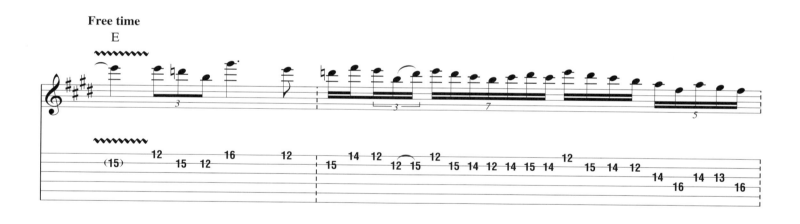

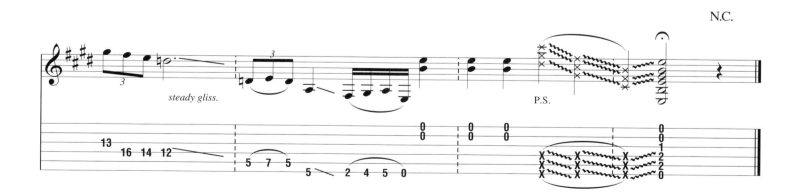

Runnin' With the Devil

Words and Music by David Lee Roth, Edward Van Halen, Alex Van Halen and Michael Anthony

Tune down 1/2 step:
(low to high) Eb-Ab-Db-Gb-Bb-Eb

Intro

Moderately ♩ = 104

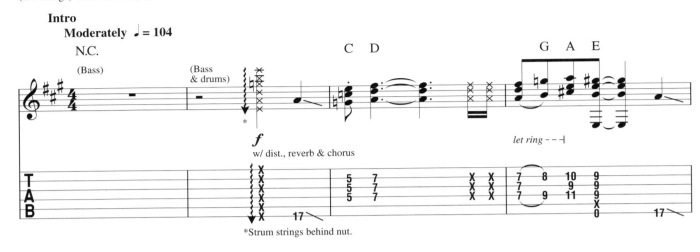

*Strum strings behind nut.

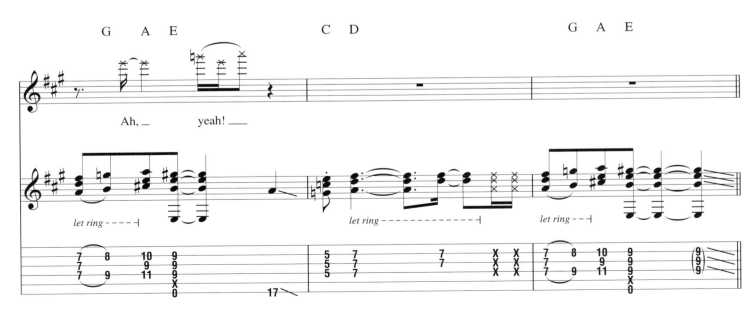

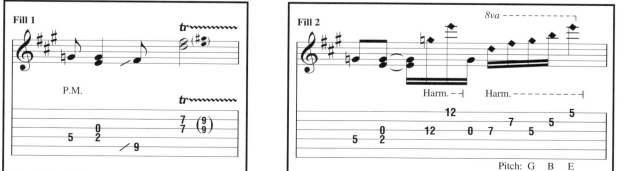

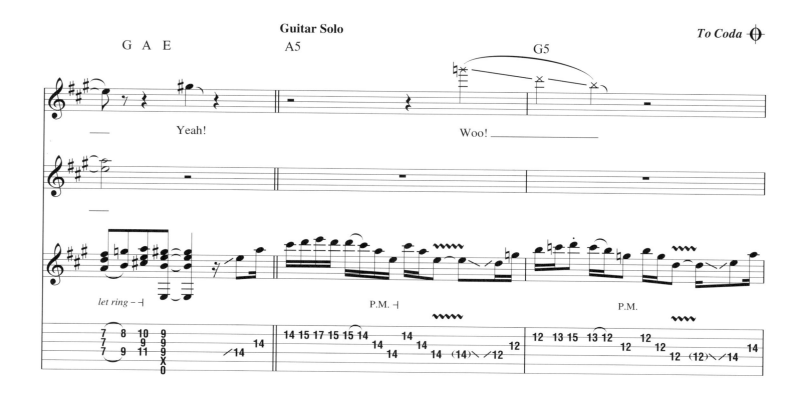

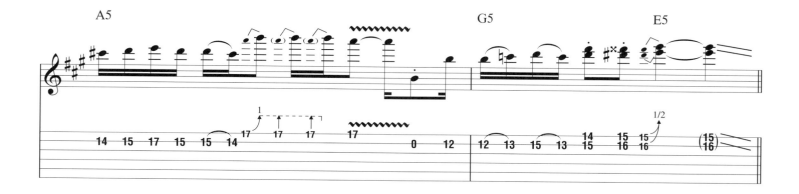

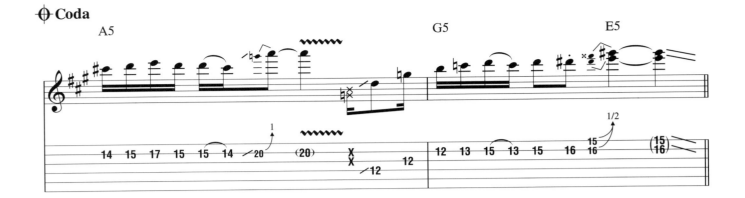

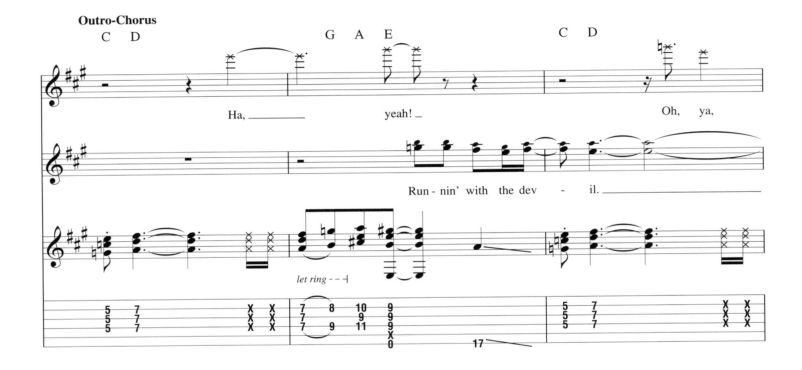

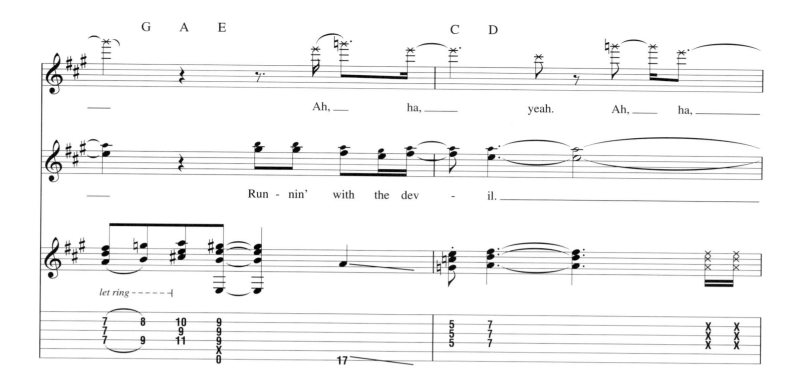

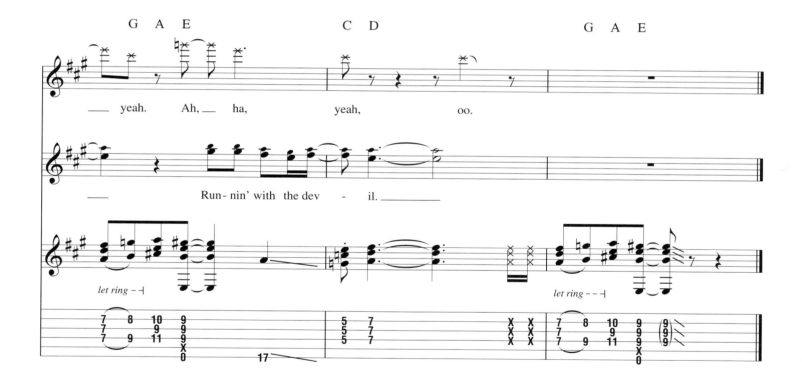

Additional Lyrics

2. I found the simple life ain't so simple
   When I jumped out on that road.
   I got no love, no love you'd call real.
   Ain't got nobody waitin' at home.

3. You know, uh, I found the simple life weren't so simple, no,
   When I jumped out on that road.
   Got no love, no love you'd call real.
   Got nobody waitin' at home.

Unchained

Words and Music by David Lee Roth, Edward Van Halen, Alex Van Halen and Michael Anthony

Drop D tuning, down 1/2 step:
(low to high) Db-Ab-Db-Gb-Bb-Eb

Intro

Moderate Rock ♩ = 138

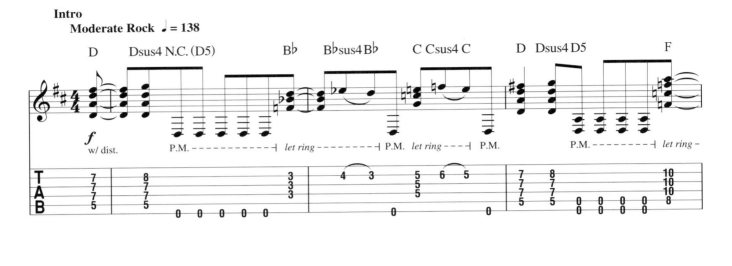

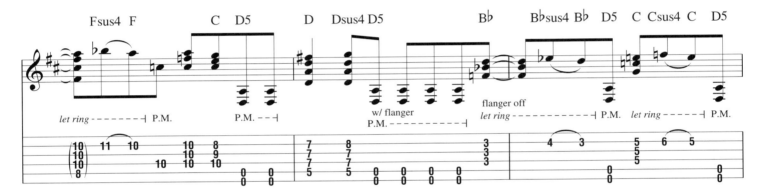

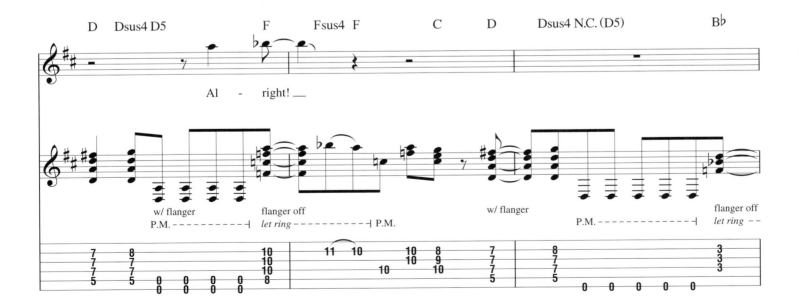

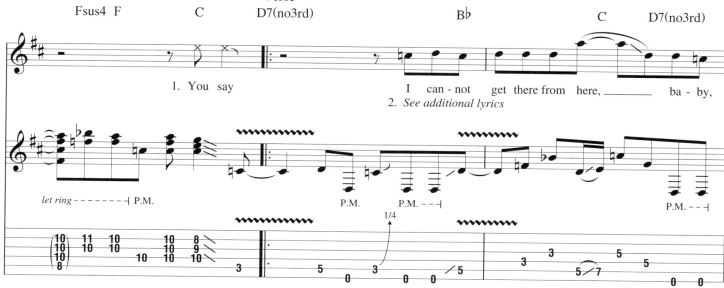

then I don't care where I'm go - in'.

Here's to your

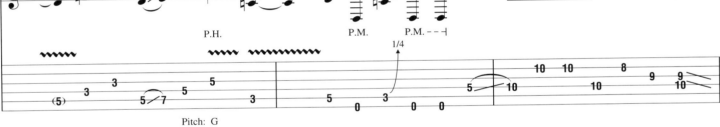

thin red line, mm, I'm step-ping o - ver.

Pitch: G

Pre-Chorus

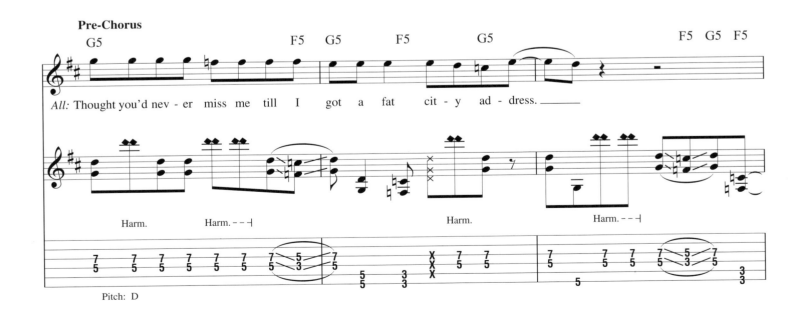

All: Thought you'd nev - er miss me till I got a fat cit - y ad - dress.

Pitch: D

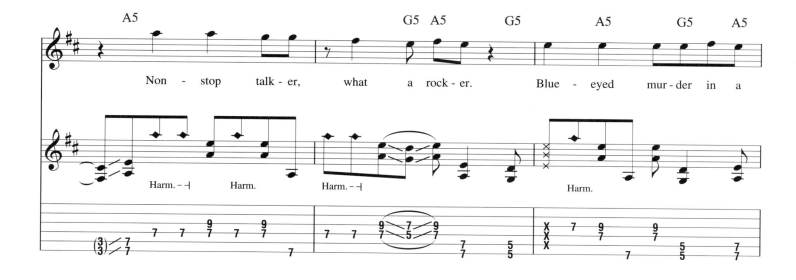

Non - stop talk - er, what a rock - er. Blue - eyed mur - der in a

Chorus

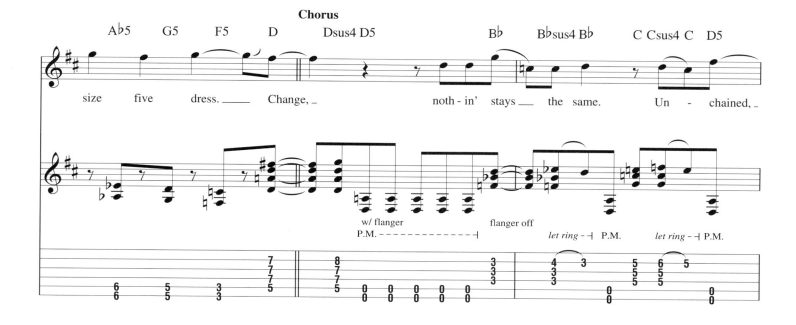

size five dress. ___ Change, _ noth - in' stays ___ the same. Un - chained, _

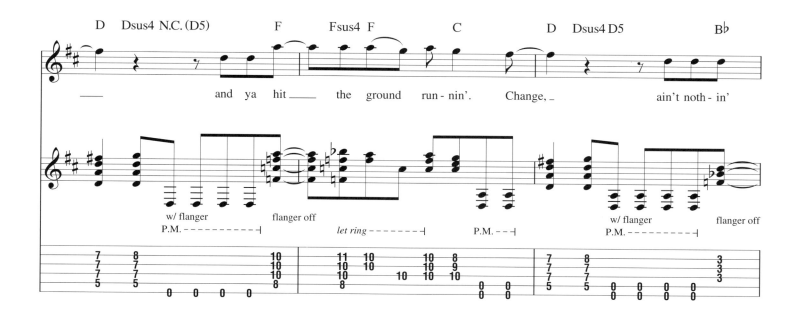

___ and ya hit ___ the ground run - nin'. Change, _ ain't noth - in'

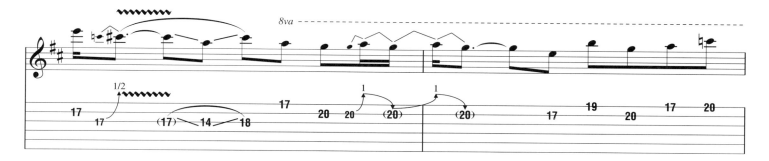

Chorus

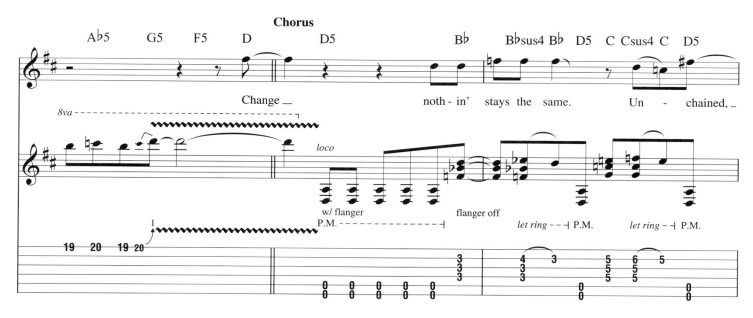

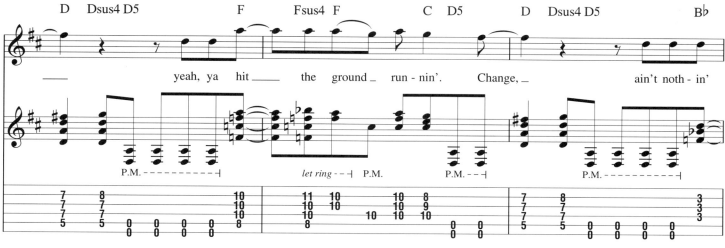

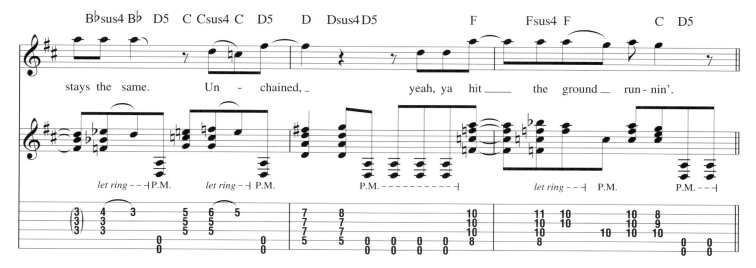

Bridge

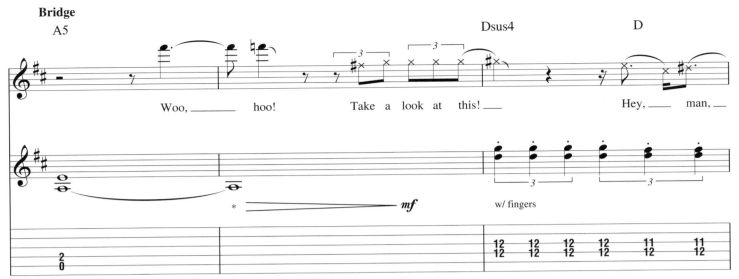

Woo, _____ hoo! Take a look at this! _____ Hey, _____ man, _____

*Lower vol. know about halfway to produce a slightly distorted tone.

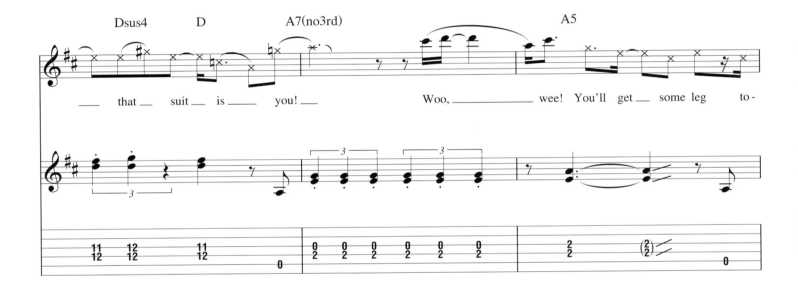

_____ that _____ suit _____ is _____ you! _____ Woo, _____ wee! You'll get _____ some leg to-

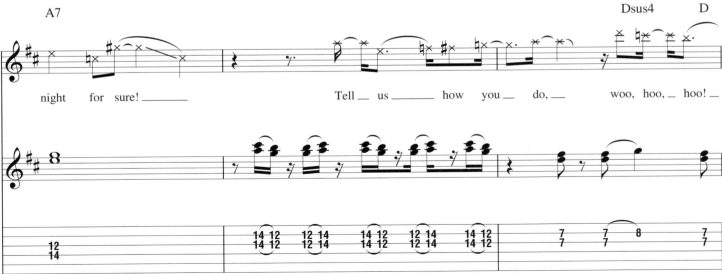

night for sure! _____ Tell _____ us _____ how you _____ do, _____ woo, hoo, _ hoo! _____

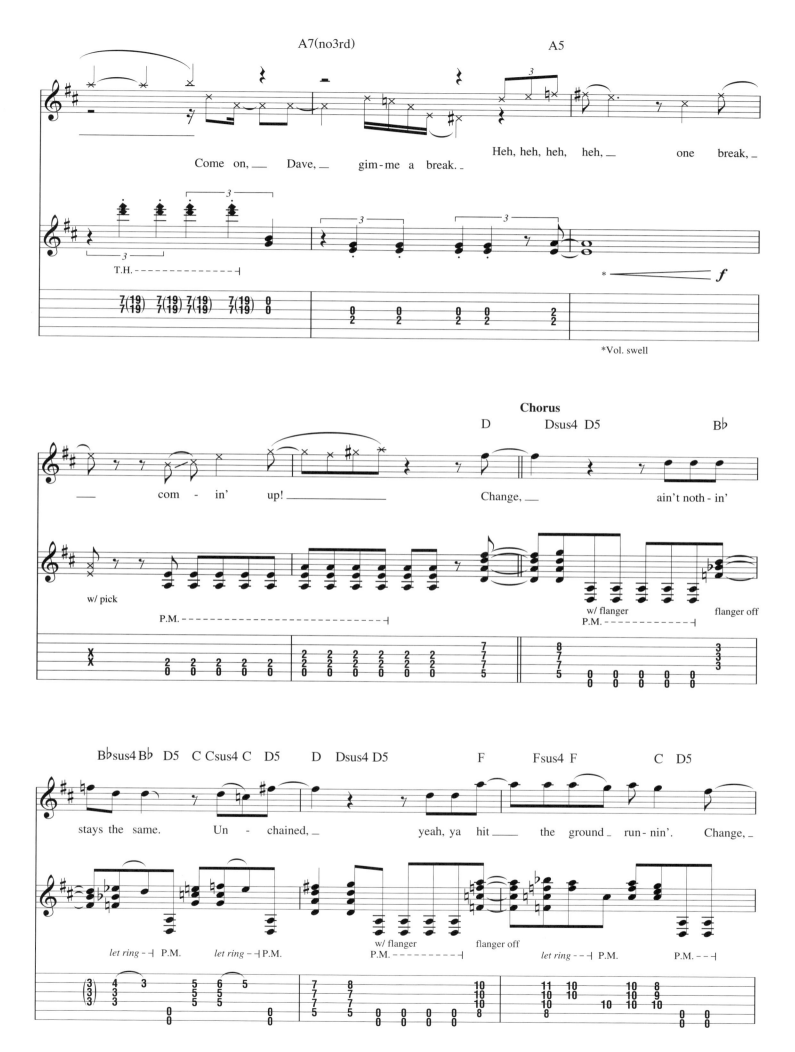

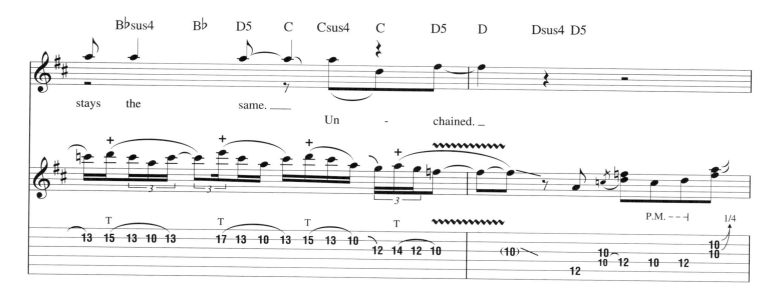

stays the same. ____

Un - chained. _

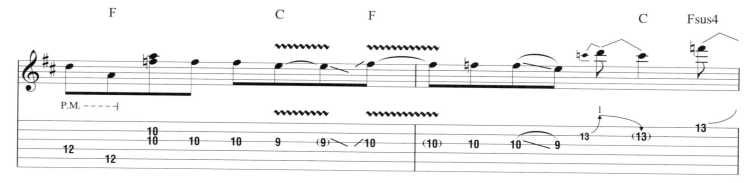

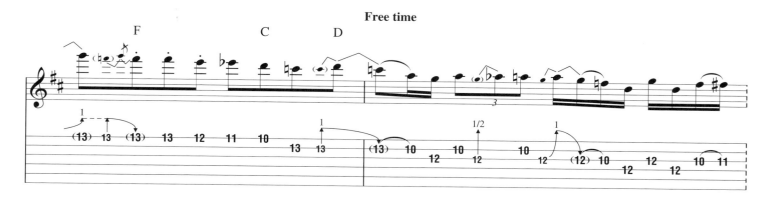

Free time

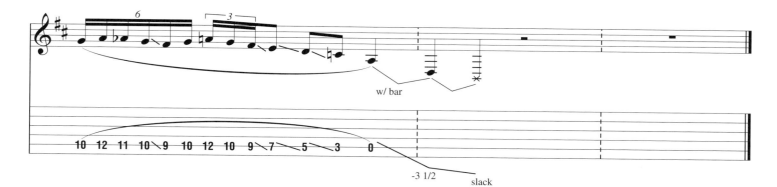

Additional Lyrics

2. I know I don't ask for permission,
   This is my chance to fly.
   Maybe enough ain't enough for you,
   But it's my turn to fly.

Yankee Rose

Words by David Lee Roth
Music by Steve Vai

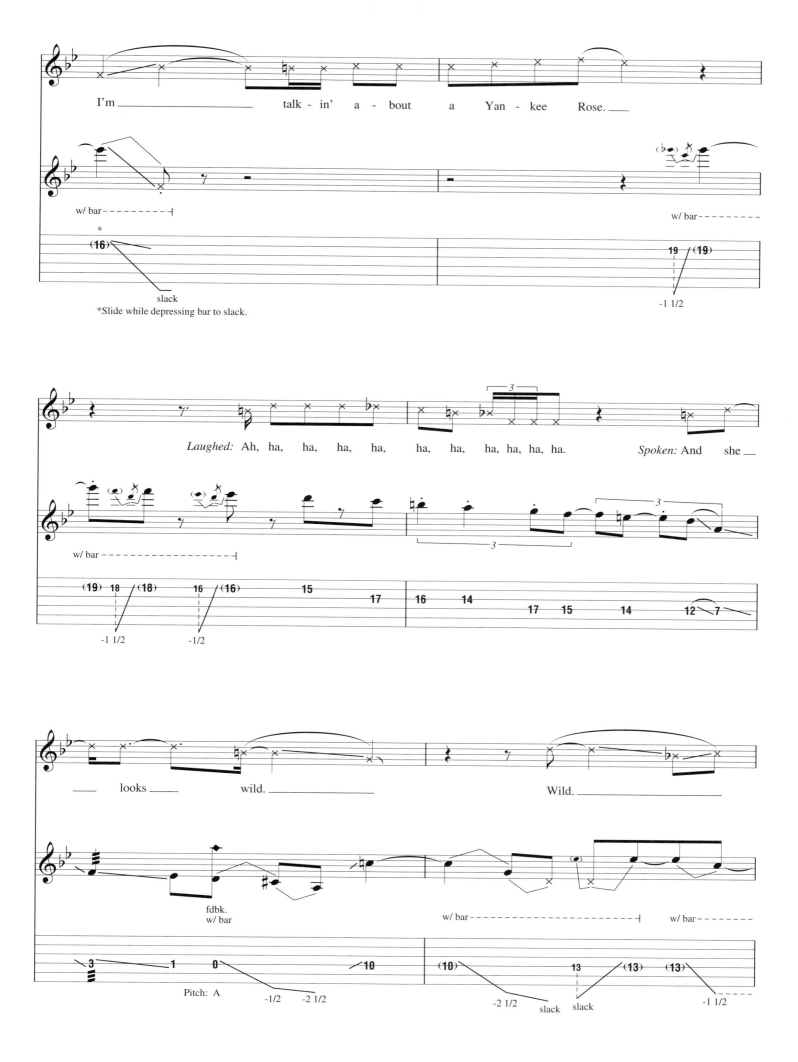

Shouted: Wild. _____

Screamed: (Wild.) _____

w/ bar -------------------

slack   slack   slack   slack   slack

§ Verse

G5

E5 F5 F♯5 G7sus4

1. Are you read - y   for   the   new   sen - sa -   tion?   Well, here's the shot   heard

2. *See additional lyrics*

wah-wah off   P.M. ------   *let ring* --------------   *let ring* --

B♭

'round the   world. _   All you back - room boys sa - lute   when her flag un - furls.

let ring --------------   P.M.   P.M.   *let ring* --

1/4 1/2 3/4 1

66

2nd time, substitute Fill 1

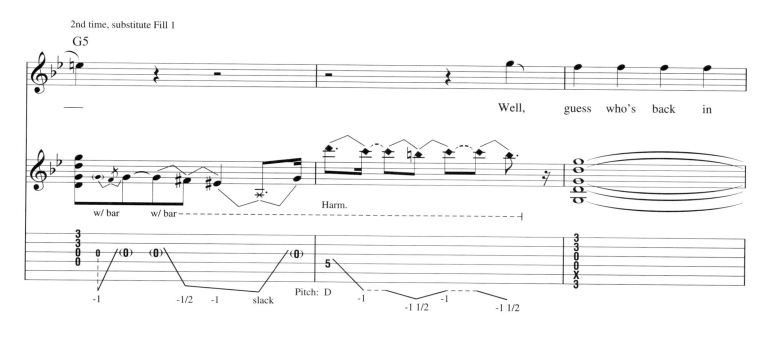

Well, guess who's back in

cir - cu - la - tion. Now I don't know what you may have heard, but what I

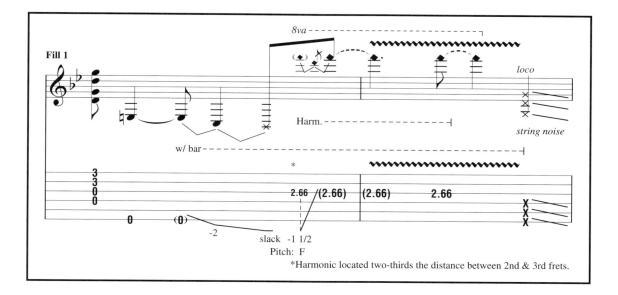

Fill 1

*Harmonic located two-thirds the distance between 2nd & 3rd frets.

Pre-Chorus

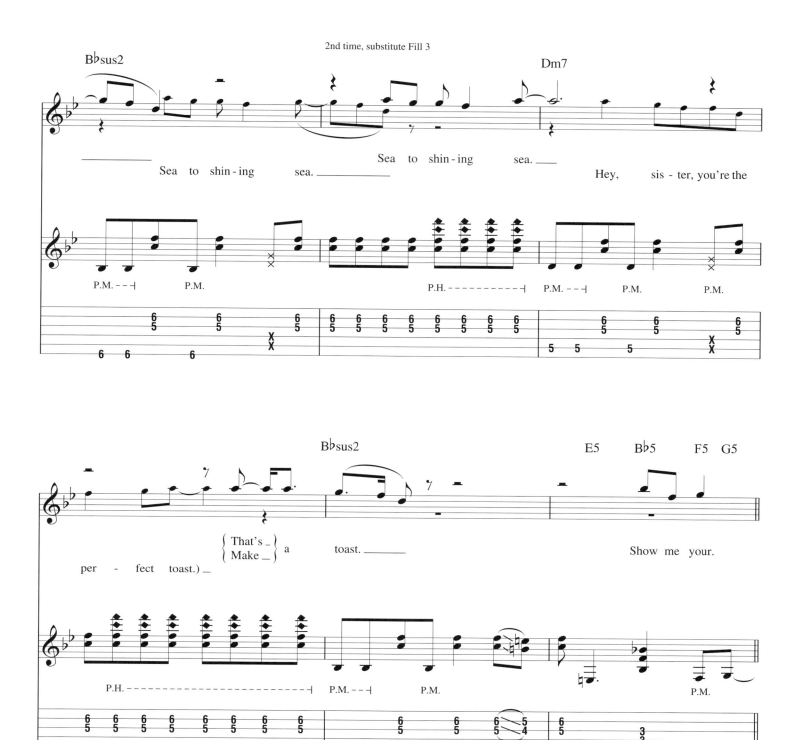

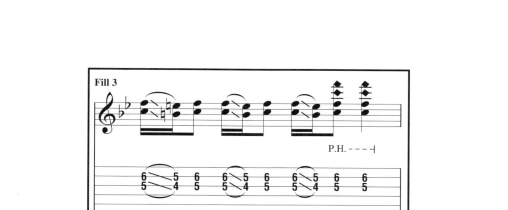

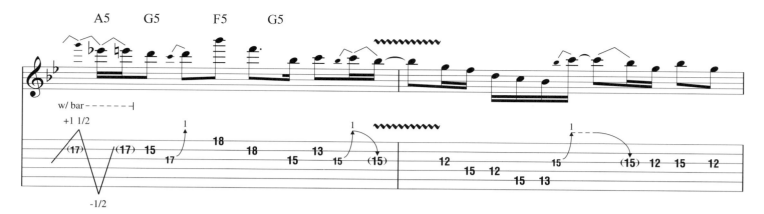

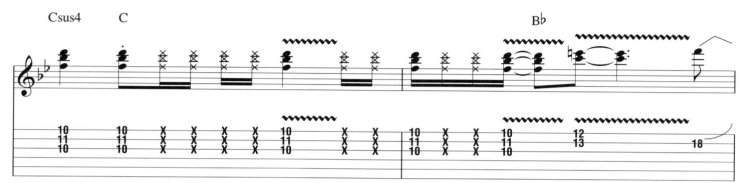

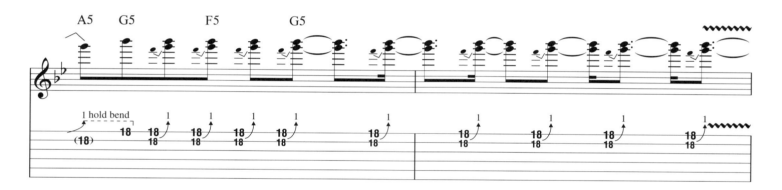

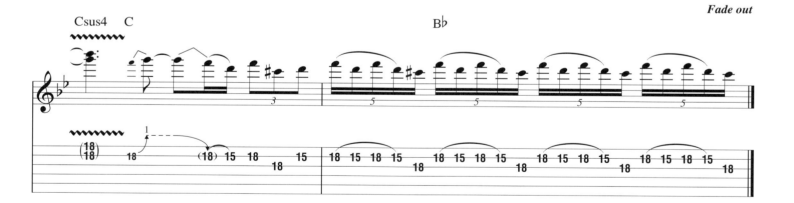

Additional Lyrics

2. When she walks, watch the sparks will fly.
   Firecrackin' on the Fourth of July.
   No sad songs tonight, something's in the air.
   You can feel it, can't ya? Whoa.
   A real state of independence.
   So pretty when her rockets glare.
   Still provin' any night that her flag's still there.

Hot for Teacher

Words and Music by David Lee Roth, Edward Van Halen and Alex Van Halen

*Pickup selector set to bridge pickup, w/ vol. control set to full vol.

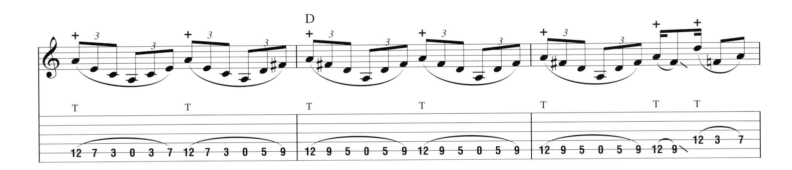

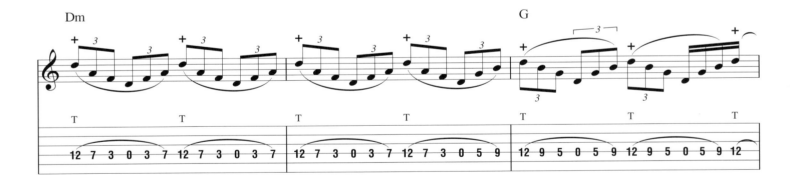

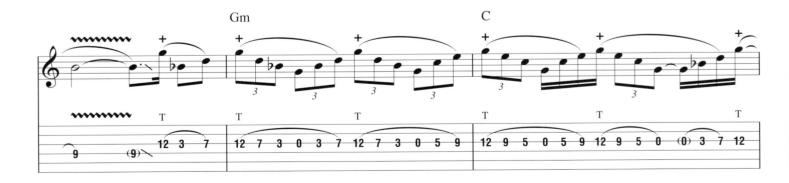

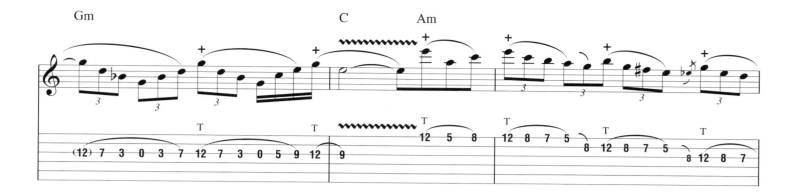

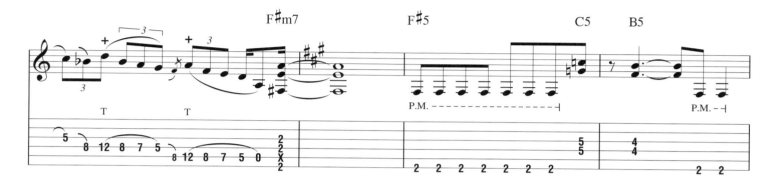

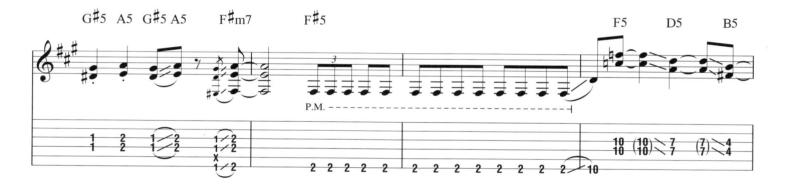

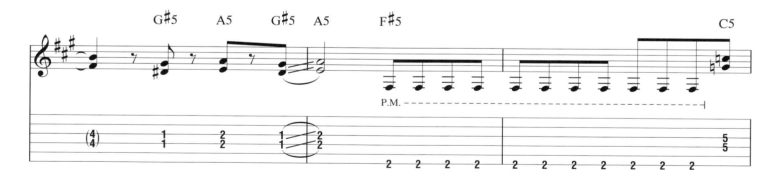

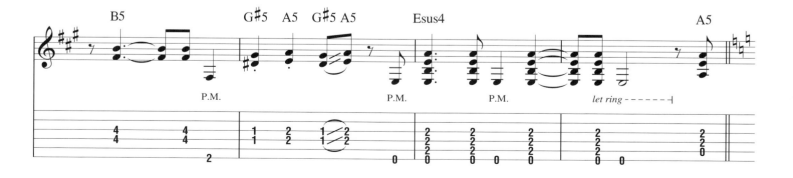

% **Interlude**

*Switch to neck pickup, w/ vol. control set to 1/2 vol.

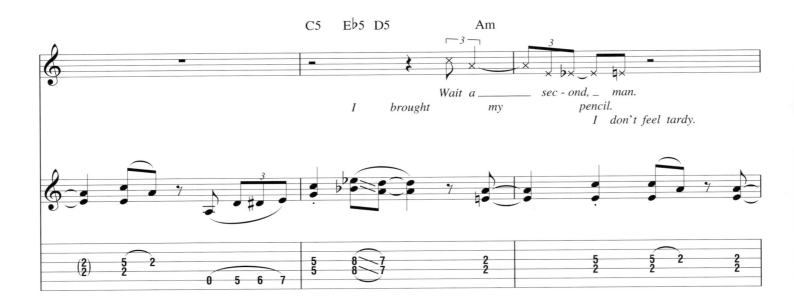

What do ya ___ think the teach - er's ___ gon-na ___ look like ___ this ___ year?
Gimme somethin' to write on,

man!

Oh! ___
Oh!

Class

(Uh!)

Uh!

dismissed!

*f
w/ pick

*Switch to bridge
pickup, full vol.

Oh, ___
Oo! ___
Oo, ___

P.M.

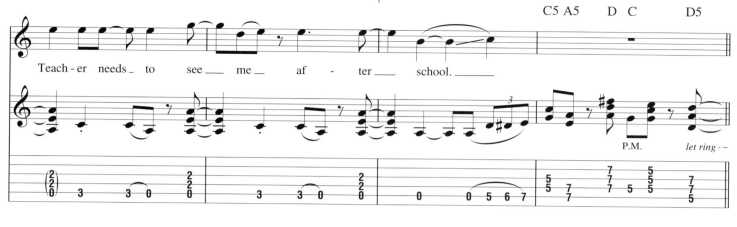

Teach - er needs __ to see __ me af - ter __ school. ____

Pre-Chorus

I think of all ____ the ed - u - ca - tion that I missed, __

*A.H.- - - - - - - - - - - -

*Artificial harmonics produced by tapping strings 12 frets above fretted notes.

but then my home - work __ was nev - er quite __ like __ this. _____

Ow! ___ Got it ___ bad _

Chorus

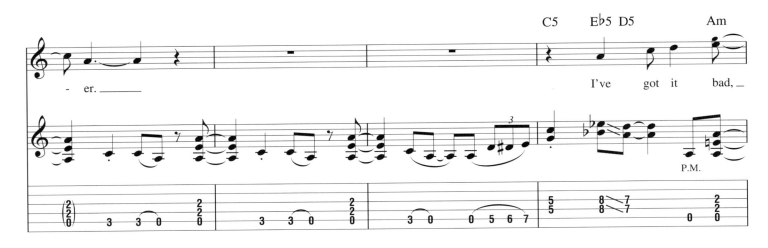

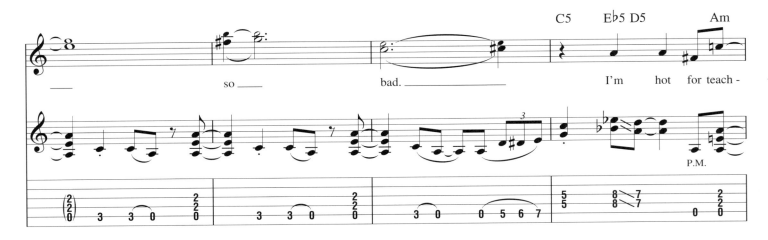

D.S. al Coda 1

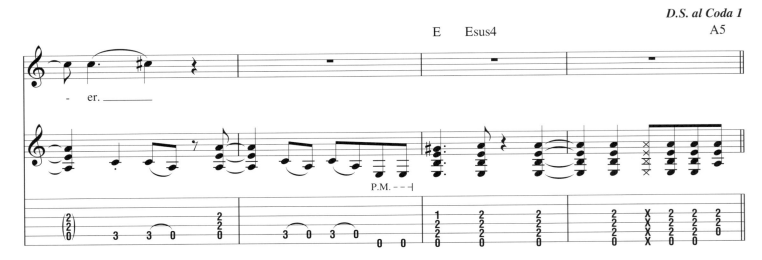

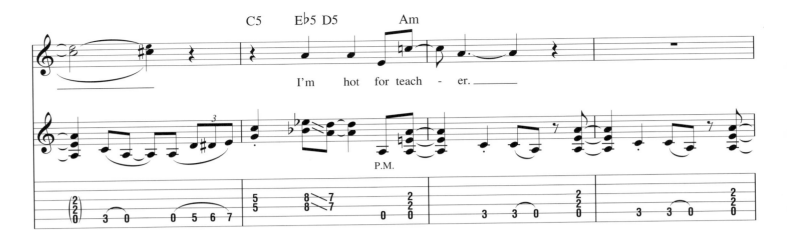

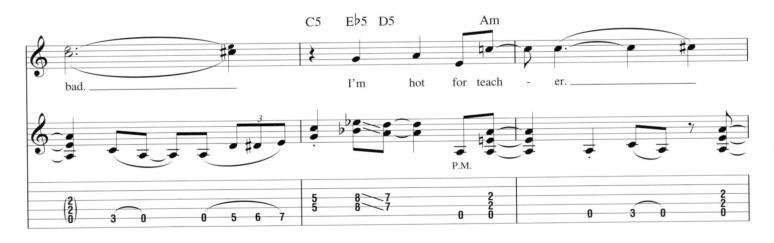

Guitar Solo

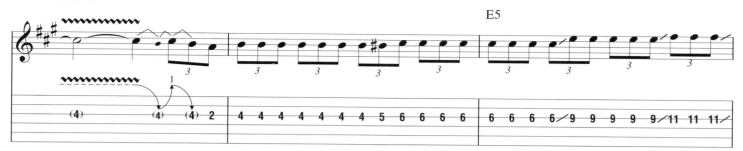

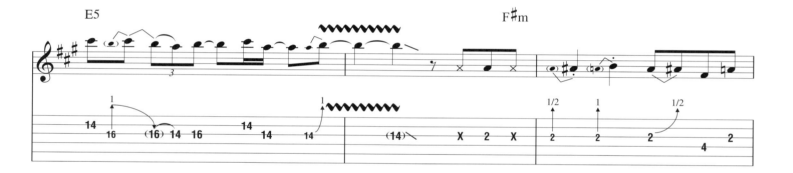

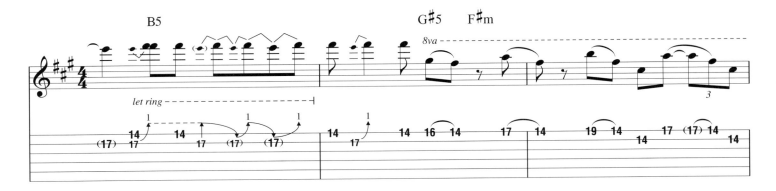

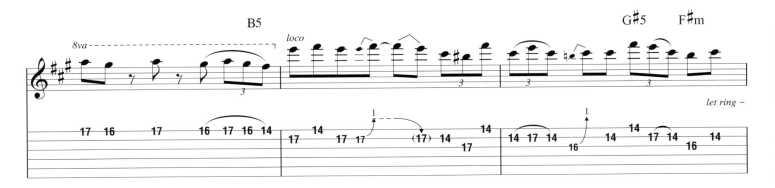

*Played as even eighth-notes.

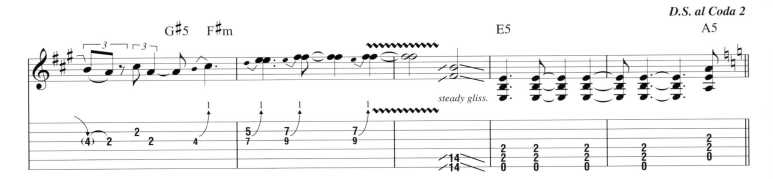

⊕ Coda 2

Chorus

I've   got it   bad, ___   got it   bad,   got it   bad. _____

I'm   hot for teach - er. _____   Oh!

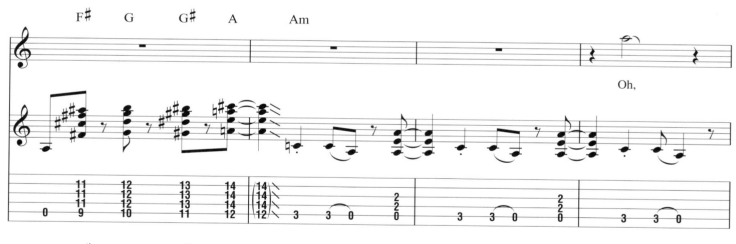

Oh,

yes, ___   I'm   hot! ___   Wow! _____

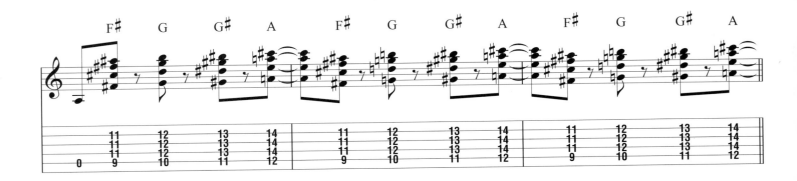

Outro
Free time

Spoken: Oh, _____ my God!

Whoo!

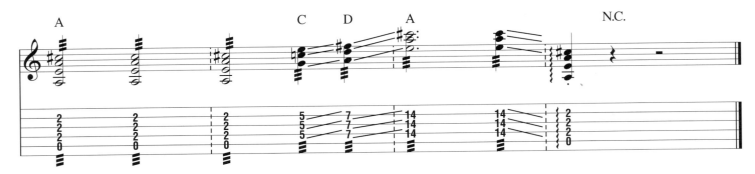

Additional Lyrics

2. I heard about your lessons but lessons are so cold.
   I know about this school.
   Little girl from Cherry Lawn, how can you be so bold?
   How did you know that golden rule?